One With God

Discipled by the Spirit

by

Carol Romeo

While every precaution has been taken in the preparation of this book, the publisher assumes no responsibility for errors or omissions, or for damages resulting from the use of the information contained herein.

ONE WITH GOD

First edition. July 20, 2024.

ISBN: 979-8224489909

Written by Carol Romeo.

Table of Contents

Introduction

Prepare yourself for a transformative season with the Lord. He yearns to fortify, uplift, and instill hope in you as you embark on a unique journey to fulfillment in harmony with God. If this year has been a struggle, He seeks to rejuvenate you. He also desires to expand you—to amplify His presence in your character. He has extraordinary plans for you because He is a benevolent God. Join me as we delve into the deeply personal experience of being one with God, a journey that is uniquely yours.

I understand that the concept of oneness with God can be challenging to grasp, and you might be uncertain about how it applies to your life. You might be wondering: What does this oneness look like? Is it something that can be achieved? What are the practical steps toward transformation? Who or what can guide me on this journey? These are all valid questions; I'm here to help you find valuable answers.

First and foremost, I want to emphasize that oneness with God is not only a concept but a reality within your reach. In the words of Jesus Himself, He expresses His intention clearly: "That they all may be one, as You, Father, are in Me, and I in You, that they also may be one in Us, that the world may believe that You sent Me. And the glory which You gave Me I have given them, that they may be one just as we are one" (John 17:21-22 NKJ). This is not a distant dream but a promise that you can hold onto in your spiritual journey, a promise of hope and assurance.

As I embark on a new season, eagerly anticipating what God has in store for me, I am mindful that many of you may be confronting new challenges in your journey. When faced with fresh beginnings, it is common practice to introspect and enter the new phase with resolutions to change A, B, or C. The challenge arises when we attempt to make these changes without seeking the Lord's counsel. Remember, His guidance is beneficial and crucial in times of change, empowering us to navigate the unknown.

The Lord has a plan for each one of our lives. He has long-range goals for us and a step-by-step plan. Plus, he wants to empower us with His Spirit so we can be successful with the outcome.

As you delve into these pages, I will unveil how we can connect to God. Numerous prayers will assist us in building our secure relationship with God. You may discover, for the first time, or through repeated applications, a facet of His character you hadn't seen before. Prayer is not just a means of communication but a gateway to a deeper understanding of God. It opens the heart, allowing God to reveal a previously hidden aspect of who He is. Our God is a fascinating God who takes delight in revealing Himself to us. As we seek Him, He is more than willing to unveil His identity to us, sparking a sense of wonder and intrigue in our hearts.

Throughout these past five decades of walking with my Lord Jesus, He has disclosed much of who He is to me. This excited my soul and spirit and drew me further into my quest to know Him more and His impassioned heart towards me. Amazingly,

I am still expanding my knowledge of God's character and experiencing new depths in my relationship with Him. I have discovered that it is a relationship that should continue to grow and mature through the years, and I invite you to join me in this journey of continuous growth.

This is my intention when compiling this book. I desire to share with you some of the ways I have learned to build a relationship with the Lord that continues to grow and expand through time. I include prayers of all sorts that reach God in various ways: prayers for healing, intercession, thanksgiving, worship, repentance, comfort, forgiveness, deliverance, meditation, praying by the Holy Spirit, and praying for the Holy Spirit. In this process, I invite you to challenge your heart and mind to expand your knowledge and experience of Jesus Christ. I have learned that God always has something more to enlighten you with.

You can begin by asking yourself, "Is my relationship with God everything I would like it to be? Have I continued to expand my heart to experience a greater measure of His love? These are good questions to explore together with the Lord."
As I did, you will find that Jesus makes it easy to respond to Him. Remarkably, it is He who calls to us to come and belong to Him. He is the one who reaches to us when we are walking in our own ways and says, "I want you to be mine." All we need to do is say yes! When I said yes to Him, I was flooded with so much love that I couldn't imagine the fullness of the relationship that was yet to come. So, I invite you, "Come with me as we explore our relationship with the Lord."

Chapter One
God's Invitation

God's grandest invitation to us is His calling to be His child. Salvation is the greatest miracle there is. Jesus decided to give up His heavenly abode to come to earth, live, and die so that we could not only know Him and His love, but He made it possible for us to become His children and live with Him for all eternity. That is miraculous! The righteousness I acquired through His action is replayed each time I need healing, peace of mind, deliverance of my fleshly habits, forgiveness of my sin, and joy in place of sorrow. The only thing that we need to do is believe in Him and follow Him. And, as we do, we come to live in the supernatural. "Incline your ear, and come to Me. Hear, and your soul shall live" (Isaiah 55:3 NKJ).

A vital ingredient to learning how to gain oneness with God is learning how to listen. Later, in this writing, I outline the steps involved with meditative prayer and explain how that practice taught me to be present with the Lord and open my heart to hear what the Lord wanted to say to me that day. Through the many years of walking with the Lord, it has been such a blessing that the Lord has found many ways to speak to and impart His heart to me.

Initially, the Spirit guided me to journal from my heart and listen as God shared His heart with me. I also found that this practice helped me listen more clearly to His voice. As I continued to surrender that time to Him, the Lord began to craft poems for me, which brought encouragement and strength to my heart. I also began to use poetry to communicate with Him. This evolved into authoring my first book, *Meditations from the River: Healing Waters for Troubled Times.*

Here is a poem from that book:

The Lord spoke: Come With Me, Child
Come, My child
Into the depths of My love.
Will it hurt?
I asked of Him.
Sometimes, He said,
But do you want to know Me?
Oh, yes, yes, I replied.
Come, take me to places
Even I have not seen.
But, I have seen them, He said.
And they are not ugly to Me
Or shameful.
They are the jewels that will
Open the doors to My love.
But, Jesus, that doesn't make sense,
I told Him.
Those dark places seem so dark.
Child, dark is really light

Through My eyes.
Will you see what I see?
Will you hold the lantern of My Spirit
And walk down with Me into the hidden places?
I will, My Lord,
But I need You to show me the way
And give me courage.
I will not fear if You are with me.
Yes, My child, yes I will be with you.
But will you choose to come?
I am calling to you.
Come to Me, come deeper, deeper still.
By Carol Romeo

Christ calls us into the deep so that our knowledge and experience of Him will deepen. He delights in uncovering the depth of our fallen nature so that He can inhabit it and fill those places with the depth of His love.

In the deep places, His love will find you! Will you answer, "Yes, Lord, I will come?"

There are many ways that God speaks to us. We just have to understand what He is saying. One of the main ways He speaks is through His Word. He speaks guidance through His Word and the promises He wants us to rehearse in our hearts. One amazing experience occurred early in my walk with the Lord. The Holy Spirit urged me to open my bible to a particular scripture. When I did, the words on the page jumped up in 3-D form. The scripture told me I would preach and write the Word of God. Even though I did not understand the whole meaning at the time, several years later, I began writing. My prior experience with that prophetic word gave me the confidence to keep writing.

This scripture fully expresses God's intention: "being confident of this very thing, that He who has begun a good work in you will complete it until the day of Jesus Christ" (Philippians 1:6 NKJ). Through His promise, I can be assured that God has not only invited us to be one with Him, but He has also invested Himself in this process:

As we reflect more on our relationship with Jesus Christ, we will find that the Word of God is essential to building an intimate relationship with Him. His words come to us from His heart as He continues to express His love to us. When we, in turn, express our love back to Him, intimacy is built between the Creator and the created. "But God, who is rich in mercy, because of His great love with which He loved us, even when we were dead in trespasses, made us alive together with Christ (by grace you have been saved)" (Ephesians 2:4-5 NKJ).

It has been such a blessing that the Lord has found so many ways to speak to me and impart His heart to me. In some of the distressing times, I found Him sitting on my bed, saying words of encouragement to still the lies within. At other times, I saw His presence wrapping around me, calming my body and soul. My Lord has creatively uncovered His intention to be near me through the years.

The scripture that I adopted as my *life promise* is Ephesians 3:16-19 (NKJ): "That He would grant you, according to the riches of His glory, to be strengthened with might through His Spirit in the inner man, that Christ may dwell in your hearts through faith: that you, being rooted and grounded in love, may be able to comprehend with all the saints what is the width and length and depth and height—to know the love of Christ which passes knowledge; that you may be filled with all the fullness of God."

Through the years, I have used that scripture as a measuring stick to see how my relationship with the Lord is doing. God has faithfully poured His love into my spirit and soul, although I have repeatedly needed to open my heart to Him. Growth in a relationship involves both parties doing the work. I have experienced God's faithfulness towards me, which, in turn, motivates me to do my part. It is the Spirit of God pouring His life into me, filling me with His joy, compassion, excitement, light, and healing, giving me all I need to respond to Him.

However, we are enriched in our relationship with Jesus and deepening our relationship with the Father and the Holy Spirit. And, as we begin this journey with them, we can share *who God is* with the world. You will discover in your journey with Him that He wants to share His love personally with you and invites you to share His love with the world. Therefore, the more we grow and take on the character of God, the more we can reflect that to others. Wherever you find yourself in your relationship with Jesus Christ, Jesus has more to impart to you. Our journey is present and eternal.

Another building block to intimacy comes from the memories we choose to focus on from our past. God's Word reminds us: "Remember His marvelous works which He has done...Remember His covenant forever, the word which He commanded, for a thousand generations" (1 Chronicles 16:12,15).

Today, I was reminded by the Spirit to remember all my lovely times with the Lord. We are often quick to remember the difficult times. Trauma has a way of impressing our minds, emotions, and even our bodies with its' identifying marks, leaving us with reminders of those occurrences. Those scars then have a way of pulling us into past pain where we can revisit the feelings and thoughts of the original experience. Satan has his hand in this process as well because he intends to divert our attention away from the goodness of God.

Here is the process I have been struggling with recently. I just turned 77 years old. I have discovered that this age has brought several challenges in my thinking. I believe that a typical thought process at this age is to look back at one's life and assess our many experiences — both good and bad. As we engage in this process, however, we need to be alerted to the focus of most of our attention. Because I still suffer from a measure of physical pain, my challenge is listening too intently to my internal lies, which draw me away from the reality of God's goodness that has rescued me all along my path.

I am grateful for the Lord's reminder that I was focusing on the *pain of the past* instead of the *praise of the past.* When I took a second look, I was so glad that I now saw the rescuing hand of God and that there was so much goodness of the Lord to delight myself in. My prayer for this season of my life has been, "Lord, I want to live this part of my life filled with the grace of God." I now see that my focus must be on Him, not on myself, to achieve that goal. Yes, there is pain in my life—quite a bit. But the goodness of God is greater than my pain. Where will I choose to focus my attention? My logical answer is "the Lord, of course." The tricky part of my task is learning how to discipline my mind and emotions to focus on God's successes and not my own failings.

Where do you go on your self-examination? You don't have to be 77 to survey your life. I have found that numerous life transitions can motivate us to observe the details of our lives. It can be a very positive process if you allow the Spirit to direct you. When you become aware of God's interventions in your life, it can bring gratitude into your heart as you rehearse God's goodness. However, we rehearse the event through the wrong-looking glass when guilt or shame pulls us along.

What memory of God's goodness extended to you will you meditate on today? Ask the Holy Spirit to guide you.

The longer I walk with the Lord, the more I recognize that there is always more goodness to discover about my Lord. A church I attended occasionally had a one-word prayer they liked to pray: "More, Lord!" To me, that says it all. Our unification with God is solidified as we communicate with each other. Prayer is vital as we seek this intimate relationship with the Lord. We can call on the Holy Spirit for the *more* we seek and for the aid He can bring to our hearts, enabling us to receive all that God wants to impart. Here is the *more* I pray for: Lord, take me higher in You. I want to live on a higher plane. I want to hear You more clearly and follow You more closely. I want my mind and heart to be set on and led by the Spirit of the Living God. The Spirit realm is right before us, but we must seek to find it. We must choose to step into our calling. This is how the Word of God describes us as we seek to fulfill our destiny:

"We have become His poetry, a re-created people that will fulfill the destiny He has given each of us, for we are joined to Jesus, the Anointed One. Even before birth, God planned our destiny and the good works we would do to fulfill it" (Ephesians 2:10).

In this process, God's directive is "come closer!" But what does that mean? When we receive Christ, His Spirit comes to live in us. So, how do we move closer? I believe Jesus wants to draw us into His heart—to discover and be impacted by the intentions of His heart. You ask, "What are the intentions of His heart?" Simply put, it is to spread His glory throughout the world. To be a part of that process, we need to connect to God's deepest desires and then be willing to carry His love, compassion, grace, and mercy to His people.

"Since Christ, though innocent, suffered in His flesh for you, now you also must be a prepared soldier, having the same mindset, for whoever has died in his body is done with sin, so live the rest of your earthly life no longer concerned with human desires but consumed with what brings pleasure to God" (I Peter 4:1-2 PT).

When I ponder the title of this work, *One with God*, I feel like there is an important issue that, if left ignored, we may miss God's intention for the oneness He intends for us. Looking at the Word of God and the recordings of Jesus' life on earth, we can see His calling is clear. His heart is focused on sharing His love and glory with the world. Even though what He accomplished was grand, He had a plan to further expand the influence of His kingdom through those people who would become His followers. That includes you and me.

It is our calling to join with God and bring His kingdom truth to the earth.

As I celebrate my oneness with You—Father, Son, and Spirit—help me remember that I am not to welcome the Spirit solely for my benefit but to welcome the Spirit to give through me. Even though our surrender to God is personal, we possess, through our actions, the ability to share His love, the knowledge of His kingdom, and exercise His authority given to us.

The *more* that God is focused on is *"more souls."* His kingdom is not relegated to building a new kingdom structure on this earth but to revealing who He is as the *Anointed One.* When Christ tells us to "love one another," it is not just a casual directive. It is His heart's cry that *all people* would come to know His

love and bring glory to Him. As His Spirit unfolds His passion for us, we are then given the privilege to join with Him in completing what He has begun.

Sometimes, however, our good intentions can become choked out through the cares of this world. Our focus, then, is on the material world rather than the spiritual one. We often have our service to the Lord tucked inside a corner of our brain, hidden from our daily cognitions. Here are some questions you can ask of the Lord to help you focus back on the spiritual: "Lord, what would you want me to do today? Are You bringing someone across my path to share Your love with?" Taking those few moments to pray can transform your day and the person or persons that He brings to you. Furthermore, I have learned how to keep one ear open to the Holy Spirit and His moment-by-moment guidance through the years.

Please try not to measure your success as big or small. Learning to pay attention to the Spirit's leading is a growth experience. What we might evaluate as small may not be small to the Lord. He might ask you, "When wronged, are you forgiving? Can you bring God's peace to someone in conflict or a smile to ease someone's pain?"

"For the Spirit teaches you all things, and what He teaches is true—it is not a lie. So continue in what He has taught you, and continue to live in Christ" (I John 2:27 NLT).

Will you pray: Dear Jesus, I am so grateful for the life You have given me and even more thankful for the new life You have given me in the Spirit. Your love and grace are beyond measure. I only ask that my heart remains open to receive what You want to pour through me. Help me to keep my focus on You and not on my material world.

As we view our heart's transformation, I will outline for you the stages of growth through which you need to travel:

- What lie has the enemy told you about who you are and what you believe about yourself? "I'm a failure. I'm worthless. I'm bad."
- Where did that lie begin? Who spoke it to you? Can you forgive the person (or persons) who said it and release any judgments against them?
- Can you forgive yourself for believing the lie and any ways that you acted on that lie?
- What wounds are you holding onto that need to be healed?
- What is the truth that the Lord says of you?

Will you pray: I thank you, Lord, that Your plans for me are perfect. Help me, Holy Spirit, to trust in God's plan. I surrender my will to align with You—Father, Son, and Holy Spirit. If I go in the wrong direction, will You correct my way?

God's directive includes an instruction to let the Spirit strip back the blockages in our hearts and minds and let the Lord transform those places. This is a stance of deeper surrender. The more we surrender to Him, the higher He can take us. We not only experience more incredible healing for our souls, but we also experience greater revelation from the Spirit.

My surrender to God led me to peace amid my pain. Fibromyalgia was my diagnosis. My journey was difficult, but the adversity significantly increased my spiritual growth. I needed to learn that even though Pain demanded my attention, my Father's voice was still more potent. In time, I discovered that God was in pain with me. This revelation expanded that truth to other areas of my life. I can't say that I perform this perfectly, although I can return to my place of peace more quickly. I am thankful that my spiritual hunger, energized by the Holy Spirit, kept me seeking and praying.

"Let us lay aside every weight and the sin which so easily ensnares us, and let us run with endurance the race that is set before us. Looking unto Jesus, the author and finisher of our faith." (Hebrews 12: 1-2 NKJ)

"For the eyes of the Lord are on the righteous, and His ears are open to their prayers..." (I Peter 3:12).

Chapter Two
Sacred Life

A divine spark ignited my sacred life as God's Spirit reached into my heart and kindled it with His miraculous saving grace—His boundless love. This revelation, a silent touch that went unnoticed by others, was a grand unveiling of God's presence. It's a moment I've revisited countless times, and its impact remains as profound as ever.

I have since discovered that the awakening I experienced set me on an exciting journey with the Lord. The Holy Spirit continues to reveal to me the truth of who God is and the power of the Spirit to live what He calls "a sacred life." As He stirs my heart, the cry that has emerged from my spirit has been, "I am in You, and You are in me." When led by the Spirit, I meditated on that phrase for one year, and the impact of that practice solidified my position in Christ. I learned that my life is found inside the person of Jesus Christ. All that makes Him holy also makes me holy. This revelation deepened my desire to align myself with His radical purpose to be made into His image.

"For whom He foreknew, He also predestined to be conformed to the image of His Son, that He might be the firstborn among many brethren. Moreover, whom He predestined, these He also called, whom He called, these He also justified; and whom He justified, these He also glorified" (Romans 8: 29-30 NKJ).

When I examine that scripture alongside my desire to be sanctified, I am reminded that it is a dual mission. This is something I can do with others. The Lord does not just give us a command and then walk away. The process of becoming "one with Christ" ("sanctification") may take time. Yes, instant miracles can come, but it is usually a step-by-step endeavor. Nonetheless, we can depend on Christ's faithfulness to walk the whole walk with us. That is an excellent reminder to keep ourselves from discouragement in the process.

In my journey towards oneness with Jesus, I've come to understand the crucial role of healing for my body, soul, and spirit. The wounds we carry from the past can mar our emotions and disrupt our communication with the Lord. Our thought processes are often tainted as well. We may have embraced falsehoods about ourselves, others, or God that we project into our present reality. These wounds can hinder our progress if we aspire to intimacy with God. Therefore, it's essential to prioritize healing. A comprehensive guide that will lead you step by step is available in my book, *Journey into Wholeness.*

You may be asking, "Where do I begin?" Looking back on our lives, it can feel like a daunting task. The place to begin, however, is the present. When the wounds of the past have not been healed, the effects of those wounds bleed into the present. You may find that your relationships are not satisfying, you act out of anger and resentment instead of love, you may have developed addictions and poor habits that you can't seem to change, or you find that it is difficult to give yourself grace in your failures and forgive others for theirs. An excellent place to start is to pray this simple prayer:

Will you pray: Forgive me for the behaviors where I acted out of the misbeliefs and how I have harmed others in this process. Lord, I bring to You the wounds of my past and the lies I believed connected to them. My healing is in Your hands, Lord. I know this transformation can't happen without you, but I am thankful that You promised to perform this work in me.

Allowing God to heal our wounds through the power of His Spirit will lead us to a place where we can present our authentic (true self) before the Lord. Our flesh selves (unhealed) usually contain the blockages to our connection with the Holy Spirit and our relationship with others. This self is motivated by worldly desires. If we choose to come into unity with Christ, however, we must allow ourselves to become vulnerable and drop the masks we have adopted to protect the fragile self. When we know that the Spirit of God covers us, there is no further need to self-protect. This can feel challenging, but if you remain connected to God, He can bring you all the grace you need to transition from your false self to your true self. The truth to apply here is that Jesus finds unity with us as we present Him with our true selves. Jesus, by His Spirit, is very willing to expose the false self, its' misbehaviors, and misbeliefs, and bring healing to those places; but, as we work together with Him, we can shed the false self and embrace the unity through which the true self will find joy.

"...that you put off, concerning your former conduct, the old man which grows corrupt according to the deceitful lusts, and be renewed in the spirit of your mind, and that you put on the new man which was created according to God, in true righteousness and holiness" (Eph. 4: 22-24 NKJ).

One thing to note is this: Sometimes, it takes a concerted effort on our part to peel back the layers of our false self and expose the true self to God. My personal journey also involved seeking out the help of a trained therapist. This is not always necessary, although my battles with abuse and depression alerted me to pursue that action. My encouragement to you is to enter into this phase of transformation prayerfully.

God alone knows how or *when* His work is complete in you. God designs your process to bring you to a conclusion that fits His perfect plan. As we travel with Him step by step, each step also arrives with His assurance that all things are under His control and that the oneness with Him that we are striving towards is His ambition. The most challenging part of applying that truth to my heart and mind comes from God's further directive to wait on His timing.

Wait! Here is the word that produces anxiety for many of us, including me.

Through many teaching sessions by the Lord, I have learned that waiting is simply a surrender to God's plan, not mine. Waiting does not come easy to our human nature but is very valuable to God's plan. Our society tells us we can get quick results, and we sometimes buy into that thinking. However, when we allow the working of His Spirit, it is by His work of grace that we can yield to His plan and not our own. When we can surrender the outcome into God's hands, this is where trust, surrender, and patience become joined together. If I become impatient over God's timetable, I often find peace when I surrender to God's will and trust His plan. Within this process, any hindrances to surrender can become visible, old wounds can surface, and misbeliefs can become known.

A helpful prayer to pray throughout this process is a prayer of thanksgiving. This prayer not only blesses the Lord, but it is always good to remind yourself that God is who He says He is and acting on your behalf. This is an excellent way to spend your wait time: confessing the good things that God is doing, even though you can't see them yet. It is praying in faith and believing in the truth of God's Word and His promises.

My prayer: Lord, I give you all my discontent and mistrust. Teach me contentment as I spend time with You. You are a God who never fails. I thank You and praise You in advance for realizing Your plans in me. Lord, thank You for being present with me now while I wait on You and Your timing."

"But let patience have its perfect work, that you may be perfect and complete, lacking nothing" (James 1:4 NKJ).

I look to the Lord to continue His work of sanctification in me. If I expressed it differently, I would say, "I want to live and demonstrate a sacred life." I have never used those words to frame my desire; nevertheless, as I write them, my heart confirms this assessment. My most profound passion as I travel this earth is "I want to leave this world better than when I arrived." I used to think this was a grandiose (self-seeking) ambition, although, as I examine the life of Christ, I discover that Jesus shared that same aspiration. If I stay connected to His plan and my longing to pursue the sacred life, I know it will be pleasing to the Lord. My pursuit of the sacred life does, indeed, line up with God's good plan for me.

Nevertheless, the term "sacred life" can invoke otherworldly imaginings, which may lead us to determine that attaining such is impossible. Let's not settle on that conclusion, however, until we look at the Word of God for its' description: "Now may the God of peace Himself sanctify you completely, and may your whole spirit, soul, and body be preserved blameless at the coming of our Lord Jesus Christ. He who calls you is faithful, who also will do it" (I Thessalonians 5:23-24 NKJ).

Will you pray: Thank you, Lord, that You are faithful. I am so glad that You are my constant God. When I become anxious with the wait, help me to remember that You are working Your good work in me even when I can't see it. Faith and trust in Who You Are become key to my ability to keep praying and believing. Thank You for Your Word, which paints a picture of Your faithfulness for me. Thank You for the many memories I possess of Your faithfulness extended towards me. I don't know what You have for me in the future, although I can be sure that Your plan for me is good!

I am proposing that you follow the guidance of the Holy Spirit and your passion to pursue oneness with God as you embrace all that it means to live a sacred life. This includes being "set apart" as belonging to the Lord. "But know that the Lord has set apart for Himself him who is godly" (Psalm 4: 3 NKJ). It also includes holiness. "Therefore, having these promises, beloved, let us cleanse ourselves from all filthiness of the flesh and spirit, perfecting holiness in the fear of God" (2 Corinthians 7: 1 NKJ). It also includes glorification. "Moreover whom He predestined, these He also called, whom He called, these He also justified, and whom He justified, these He also glorified" (Romans 8: 30 NKJ). God initiates the work of living a sacred life, although we are called to continue the work that God began. "And do not be conformed by this world, but be transformed by the renewing of your mind, that you may prove what that good and acceptable and perfect will of God is" (Romans 12: 2 NKJ).

As you follow that directive by God, what is God speaking to you? What wounds or hindrances have limited your pursuit of intimacy with the Lord? Can you offer those areas to God? Even though you have a part to play in aligning yourself with God's plan for oneness with Him, God is still faithful to meet you and heal the places that continue to trip you up.

This season can be the most challenging for you, but it also can be where you have experienced your most significant growth. When you examine your false self and some of your troublesome behaviors, try not to shame yourself. Shame and guilt can produce internal messages like: "You are bad, worthless, You can't do anything right." The truth is, "God is not discouraged when we bring Him the impure parts of our hearts." God created us with Christ rooted in our identity, and He never loses sight of His plan, even when what we offer Him is some of the unlovely parts of our hearts. He can transform us into our true selves, living from the guidance and power of the Spirit and not from fleshly desires.

Pride, self-aggrandizement, pursuit of financial gain, demeaning others, and mistrust of God must be released to God in exchange for trust in God's faithfulness, promises, protection, forgiveness, righteousness, and kingdom. The scripture below shows that part of our calling is to join with God and bring His kingdom truth to the earth.

This is Jesus' directive to His disciples: "And as you go, preach, saying, The kingdom of heaven is at hand. Heal the sick, cleanse the lepers, raise the dead, cast out demons. Freely you have received, freely give" (Matthew 10: 7-8 NKJ).

You may ask, "What kingdom are we preaching about?" If our understanding is incomplete, we may perceive that God and we live in two separate worlds. God lives and rules from His spiritual kingdom in heaven and in our material world. Unless we deepen our understanding of what the joining together of our two separate kingdoms looks like, we might abandon the proposal. Once again, we need to look to the Word of God for the answers to our dilemma. Jesus gives us further directives regarding His kingdom as He teaches us to pray:

"Our Father in heaven, Hallowed be Your name. Your kingdom come, Your will be done on earth as it is in heaven" (Matthew 6: 9-10 NKJ).

Through this scripture, we learn that we bring the kingdom of God to earth through the activity of the Holy Spirit, which works in and through us. Kingdom living is not only ours to enjoy here on earth but also ours to give away. We have the same Holy Spirit living in us who worked signs and wonders through Jesus Christ when He walked this earth. "Therefore, since we are receiving a kingdom which cannot be shaken, let us have grace, by which we may serve God acceptably with reverence and godly fear" (Hebrews 12: 28 NKJ).

My challenge to you is that you would examine your heart before God and write out your desires from your authentic self. "I thank you, Lord, in advance of Your plan for my transformed heart." Let this poem be your prayer.

A NEW HEART
I lay my heart open to You.
I lay it on the altar.
Take it in Your hands, my Savior,
And shape it and change it—
Enlarge it.
Take the fear that lies within
And the hurts,
The callused and stony places—
Make them soft,
Pliable in Your Hands.
Do with me what You will
For I am Yours.
You are the Lord that changes not—
Change me.
Mold me into Your image, Lord.
Change me into Your shape.
Make my will Yours.
For I desire to be like You,
To walk Your way,
The path that You have laid
Before me.
My Savior
Press Your life into mine.
Make me Yours.
By Carol Romeo

One new direction that God is speaking to me has been both rewarding and challenging. Isn't that true of the many instructions that God gives? When we are asked to open our hearts and look inside, the vision can be alarming and yet promising when we see the healing that God wants to bring. At this moment, God's directive was to simply still myself before Him. It sounded simple enough, although, in my practice, I discovered some flesh desires that needed to be challenged and healed to pursue my goal of the sacred life.

I found that the more I quieted myself, the greater a nagging belief intruded on my thinking, "Life is passing me by. I am missing something that can't be retrieved." What exactly do I think I am missing? Success? Being known? I hate to think that those beliefs are still a part of me. Nevertheless, I am willing to surrender those misbeliefs to the Lord.

While active in my prior dancing career, those beliefs were the ones that kept me motivated. Yes, they were the beliefs that helped me succeed in my career, but the Lord encouraged me to change. The success I am in search of now is spiritual gain. The intention of my heart needed to shift from a worldly pursuit (with my focus on self and the needs of the flesh) to a sacred quest (with my focus on God and His heart's desires). In my sacred pursuit, I knew that growth in the Spirit was an intricate part of the journey. As I continued in prayer, the Holy Spirit taught me the steps needed to align myself with God's sacred calling. I knew sanctification was essential to my new identity, but what does aligning myself with God's holy calling mean? I found a new level of surrender that the Lord was calling me into—His plan vs my plan. As I pressed into the new thing God had for me, I was surprised by the flood of peace and joy flowing into my heart. The hunger that was then birthed in my soul was beckoning me to keep coming, and as I did, I noticed that God's desires were making their way into my heart, producing the oneness with God I had been longing for.

Chapter Three
The Character of God

As we "become one with Christ," we take on the character of God. What does that look like? Let's look at the examples of Christ in His Word. As we examine each of His character references, we also discuss the character traits in yourself that you desire to be transformed. This change often begins with your awareness of the desired change and surrendering to God for His help and guidance.

Get ready for a great season with the Lord. He wants to strengthen, encourage, and empower you with His Spirit so you can have a successful outcome. He also wants to enlarge you—to enlarge His life in your character. He has great things for you because He is a good God.

As we search for the character of God, we will also examine our specific needs as we travel through our various seasons with the Lord and God's role in gratifying those needs. There is a strength in the character of God that will be present to meet all your needs. As I outline our various needs, I will also reveal the role of God as He meets those needs. I am using the next outline to examine each of our needs, the conflict that can be present, the central question concerning the nature of God, and the name (identity) of God: How God is revealing Himself at that stage.

Stage One God : Protector

- Need: safety, survival
- Conflict: Is God a rewarder or a punisher?
- Central Question: In a world full of danger and chaos, is God a good God?
- Name of God: Good Shepherd: Jesus spoke, "I am the good shepherd. The good shepherd gives His life for the sheep" (John 10:11).

Will you pray: Lord, You say that You are the Good Shepherd. In the chaos of my life, will You meet me? I long to trust Your protection as I lean into You.

Stage Two God: Covenant

- Need: belonging
- Conflict: worldly fulfillment or obedience to God
- Central Question: Is God a personal God? (Will God hear and answer MY prayers?)
- Name of God: Almighty "When Abram was ninety-nine years old, the Lord appeared to Abram and said to him, I am Almighty God; walk before Me and be blameless and I will make My covenant between Me and you, and will multiply you exceedingly" (Genesis

17:1-2).

Will You pray: Help me to receive Your promise that You are with me. When I obey You, will You draw me close to You?

Stage Three God: Redeemer

- Need: forgiveness of sins/worth
- Conflict: self-righteousness or shame vs unconditional love
- Central Question: Will God be good to me in my sin?
- Name of God: Jesus the Savior "And she will bring forth a Son, and you shall call His name JESUS, for He will save His people from their sins" (Matthew 1:21).

Jesus, I have sinned against You in many ways. Your Word says that You are a forgiving God. Will You cleanse me with Your righteousness?

Stage Four God: Peace

- Need: Internal peace
- Conflict: anxiety vs. peace
- Central Question: How can I be in the world and not of it? (Is God able to keep me?)
- Name of God: Prince of Peace: "For unto us a Child is born, unto us a Son is given...And His name will be called Wonderful, Counselor, Mighty God, Everlasting Father, Prince of Peace" (Isaiah 9:6).

God, I am anxious over so many things, but I pray that this is not Your plan for me. Help me to step into Your peace and leave my worries to You.

Stage Five God: Creator

- Need: to partner with God as co-creator in one's life
- Conflict: to align with God's will (destiny) vs. ego intentions (self-importance)
- Central Question: Does God want to communicate with me?
- Name of God: Creator (God created man in His image. We are the only members of creation who can reason with God.) "And the Lord God formed man of the dust of the ground and breathed into his nostrils the breath of life, and man became a living being" (Genesis 2:7).

Will you pray? I know that You are my Creator, yet there are times when I lose sight of Your plan, and I long to partner with You in Your transformation of my life. Help me to align my desires with Your plan.

Stage Six God: Healer

- Need: to experience God
- Conflict: the battle between seeing with our spiritual eyes (kingdom living) or trusting in the material world.
- Central Question: Is God a supernatural God? (Does He heal today?)
- Name of God: Physician (Jesus stood in the temple

and declared Himself as physician.) Jesus, speaking of Himself, said, 'The Spirit of the Lord is upon Me because He has anointed Me to preach the gospel to the poor; He has sent Me to heal the brokenhearted, to proclaim liberty to the captives and recovery of sight to the blind..." (Luke 4:18).

Will you pray: You are the only one, Lord, who can open my spiritual eyes. I want to join You and bring the gifts of Your Spirit to this earth. I am grateful You are a supernatural God who longs to bring that to Your people.

Stage Seven God: Pure Being

- Need: unity with God (transcendence) and unity with one another
- Conflict: how to transcend the limitations of humanity, time, and space
- Central Question: How big is our God?
- Name of God: I AM, "And God said to Moses, I AM WHO I AM. And He said, Thus you shall say to the children of Israel, I AM has sent me to you" (Exodus 3:14).

Will you pray: God, I desire to be one with You. Will you show me how big You are? Join Your life into mine and impart to me the broadness of Your kingdom that is available to me right now in my present state.

As you work through these stages, you will discover that in the character of God, there is the ability to meet your every need. Trusting and resting in His character brings rest to your soul, and you can also learn how to incorporate that character trait into your character. Hence, there comes a more profound togetherness with the Lord. If our goal is to be one with God, we need first to become aware of His character and then recognize the integration He wants to bring to us as we merge His image into our own.

This is an amazing happening: As we meditate on the personhood of God, those Godly responses of the Lord are transferred into the making of our new spiritual being. Prayers of thanksgiving are one way we can aid this process. Through the years, God has revealed to me that He is never far from me. As I travel, He is forever at my side. For that, I can be thankful. I can be thankful for His constant presence. I can be thankful that He is working His goodness in and through my character. I can be thankful that He knows the path He is leading me on (even when I can't see it) and that it is for my good.

"The fruit of the Spirit is love, joy, peace, longsuffering, kindness, goodness, faithfulness, self-control" (Galatians 5:22-23 NKJ).

One day, while I was praying, Jesus revealed a picture of a shiny silver goblet with delicately carved handles on either side. I thought to myself that it had the appearance of a winner's cup, a trophy. And the Lord said, "That's right, and this is you," As I watched Him, He held me up and displayed me before all the hosts of heaven (particularly in the face of the enemy) as a winner—an overcomer. I questioned, "How can He label me as a winner?" I certainly did not feel like a winner.

Then I stood on tiptoe and peered over the lip of the cup, down into the deep chalice, and what I saw was blood—His blood. My heartbeat excitedly as I gave credence to His message, "I was an overcomer because of the blood of the Lamb that filled me, His vessel."

I watched as He, the Master-craftsman, continued to elevate me, the silver goblet, His masterpiece, before Himself when an image appeared on my surface. It was His image that was being reflected. I was amazed, although my amazement was drawn inward as I reflected on my internal state. "Where did my shame go?" I asked. He whispered, "What shame? All I see is My glory!" Will you let His glory transform your shame? He longs to make you a winner!

"For in Christ the fullness of God lives in a human body, and you are complete through your union with Christ" (Colossians 2:9-10 NLT).

As we look at the character of God, we also need to look at how God sees us. The above picture of the silver goblet is an excellent example of this. He longs for us to know ourselves through His eyes (replacing our lies). God, the Father, sees us through the person of His Son Jesus. This is meant to be an encouragement to myself and all of you. God labels us in many ways: "Child of God." "A light to the world." "Peacemakers." "Beloved." "Apple of His eye." "One with God." "Chosen One." "Disciple. "Forgiven One." It is up to us to remind ourselves of **who** we are and that we are the ones God has sent to spread our good fortune to the world. Our ultimate calling is to bring our transformed being to those who do not know Jesus.

Jesus states this to the Father, "As You sent Me into the world, I also have sent them into the world" (John 17:18).

Through the past 47 years of walking with the Lord, He has taught me so much about what it means to join with Him in ministering His light to the world. It has been an exciting adventure. He has created many different opportunities for me to speak His Word to others, display God's image to others, impart God's love to others, teach others through my books, and give to others at their point of need; the Lord is so creative. When we join with Him, He transforms our lives and plants us in His body, where we can participate with Him and see the transformation of others.

So, what is the Lord asking of us? He is sending us into the world as His representatives. With our eyes on Him and His kingdom, we can bring His kingdom to the earth. When Jesus was sent, He did not transform the world's view—He came to demonstrate the practices of another kingdom. His example was a radical heart reform and not a worldly reform. We can't expect the world to look like us, but we can expect ourselves to look like Jesus. We live in a different kingdom even while planted on this earth.

Will you pray? God, grant me Your Spirit to pray according to Your Word. By Your grace, uncover the thoughts and prayers in Your heart. I desire to join my heart to Yours and see the fulfillment of Your prayers.

Chapter Four
Prayer

Seeing through the eyes of Jesus is an optimal way to gain oneness with God. When we see His compassion for others, we can learn to have eyes to view the pain of others. In this chapter, I will outline the many prayers that can lead us to know the heart of God. One of the ways to become "one with God" is by drawing close to Him through the prayers we offer to Him. You will see that opening your heart in prayer provokes a joining together with the Spirit of God and oneness with God. In fact, it is the Spirit of God who teaches us to pray in unison with the Lord. God is excited to share with us what is on His heart. I invite you to allow the Spirit to uncover just what you need to aid your understanding and your heart's response to your pursuit of intimacy with God.

"By this, we know that we abide in Him, and He in us, because He has given us of His Spirit" (I John 4:13 NKJ).

My journey with the Lord is defined mainly through my prayer life. Early after my dedication to Jesus, my hunger to connect more deeply to Him led me into a quest to gather all the knowledge I could about connecting to Him in prayer. I persevered in my practice of applying the knowledge I was gaining to my ongoing relationship with God. The payoff was wonderful. Jesus came and met me all through my personal times with Him. The oneness that I started experiencing with Him satisfied my soul and increased my hunger, once again, for more of Him.

As I thought more about prayer, the Lord painted a picture of how He viewed it. He said, "Prayers are like the flowers I created. They are as varied as the array of brilliant colors that paint your landscapes in the spring and summer seasons. They are sweet-smelling as they rise from your lips to bless Me. The scent of your love arouses me, and your attention draws Me to come close to you.

Each prayer is also a seed, which the Lord plants inside the soil of His heart. He is attentive to water it by the washing of His Holy Spirit. He shines His light upon the budding sprout, nourishing and bringing it to life. In His wisdom, He waits and watches for the right timing to bring forth the flourishing flower.

The flower is stunning, but His work is not finished. He tends the garden with His own caring hands, pruning the plants when needed to enhance their growth and maturity. He takes great delight in walking in His garden or sitting in His home by an open window overlooking His amazing floral design. His vision brings much joy to His heart as His eyes remain fixed on the blooms now opened wide before Him.

Let this illustration be replayed in your mind and spirit as you form the many prayers inside you. These scents are ready to bless the Lord as He draws you to Himself. Even though our prayers are varied, they all have one thing in common—they all lead us on the journey of meeting with our God.

"For the eyes of the Lord are on the righteous, and His ears are open to their prayers..." (I Peter 3:12).

Nevertheless, before my movement towards acceptance and throughout my many years of struggling with physical pain, I have lifted before God many varied types of prayers. From my desperation, some prayers became mingled with my tears and shouts that escaped from the deepest valleys of my sickened soul. Some prayers were birthed from the anger and anguish in my heart, the desperation in my darkened soul, and the unbelieving prayers.

As you can see, my prayers were not always initiated by the Spirit. Even through my desperate prayers, God saw my seeking heart and led me to connect with Him. Sometimes, the way we pray is not the important thing. The important thing is that we do pray. As we reach out to God in whatever way we can, He is faithful in reaching out to us.

That is the wonderment of God! By His Spirit, He can travel into the hidden recesses of the heart and discover the prayers that we are either afraid to speak or have no knowledge of ourselves. I am so thankful that He searches for the good intention that is sometimes buried beneath the fear and anguish. His loving heart carries these prayers into His heart and responds to us. Amazing, isn't it?

"Likewise, the Spirit also helps with our weaknesses. For we do not know what we should pray for as we ought, but the Spirt Himself makes intercession for us with groanings which cannot be uttered. Now He who searches the hearts knows what the mind of the Spirit is because He makes intercession for the saints according to the will of God" (Romans 8:26-27).

As I gave place to the Spirit of God to lead me in my next season of prayer, there were many new directives He brought to my prayers, which then engaged me in a prayer life pleasing to God. What a privilege it is to join with the Lord and breathe the prayers dear to Him. When we can glimpse what this calling that He has placed on us means, we will be overjoyed to run into that secret place and kneel together with Him. The spiritual awakening I received from the Spirit, together with my desperation to connect more deeply with the Lord, kept me engaged in the prayer process.

Shortly after being introduced to the Holy Spirit, He began to teach me about intercessory prayer. What a glorious season that was. It felt like my heart was being drawn into His, and I got a peek at the burdens weighing on His heart. Our Lord is faithful to carry the concerns troubling our souls. We can see multiplied examples of those actions as Jesus walked this earth. He carried our burdens to the cross with Him. And He continues to make intercession for us as He is seated in heaven. Furthermore, we are instructed to do the same.

In one of my prayer times, the Holy Spirit gave me a picture. I saw a sea of broken and battered children (of all ages) that extended in all directions as far as my eye could see. At the same time, I began to feel the heart of God for them. The grief was so severe that I wept together with the Lord for over an hour. When the grief began to lift, I asked the Lord what He wanted me to know about that time. He told me, "I am sending you to minister to the broken, but first, I must give you My heart for them." I learned an important lesson that day. Our ministry must pour forth from God's heart.

Following this experience and throughout my ministry to the broken, I encountered the heart of God: His compassion, love, grief, sadness, and comfort. In my inspiration to be one with God, the impact of His heart upon my heart was significant. This poem is a reminder to me that all I needed to do was lean into His loving heart and trust in the promise of God for me and those I minister to.

The Promise of God

Child, call upon Me in the night
When sorrow dims the brightest light,
When cares wake you from your sleep,
Call on Me, your cares I'll keep.
When trouble tugs at every side
Draw close to Me, and there abide.
In My heart of hearts, you'll find
Solace for your troubled mind.
Bring to Me your thoughts, your worries.
I am not a God who tarries.
I will answer when you call.
You don't need to carry all.
Let Me settle and sustain you.
Give to Me the fears that drain you.
Do not keep Me from your strife.
Freely give Me of your life.
Trust Me, child, to be beside you,
There to care for and to guide you.
I am there with you today.
That is where I'll *always* stay.
By Carol Romeo

In response to God's promise and from a heart of trust, I searched my heart to release my burdens to the Lord. Simultaneously, I was drawn into prayer for those I was ministering to. I experienced the heart of God as it was poured out through me to bring the power of His healing to those who needed it. Partnering with God in this manner also brought healing to my heart. This encounter also ushered me into a season of intercessory prayer, where the excitement generated by the activity of the Holy Spirit became mine.

"Finally, my brethren, be strong in the Lord and in the power of His might. Put on the whole armor of God, that you may be able to stand against the wiles of the devil...praying always with all prayer and supplication in the Spirit, being watchful to this end with all perseverance and supplication for all the saints" (Ephesians 6:10-11).

I am so thankful to the Holy Spirit for stirring my heart and spirit in this pursuit. He placed a passion in my heart for intercessory prayer. Under His guidance, I prayed for people I knew and people I didn't know. I prayed for nations and salvation for those who did not yet know the Lord. As my prayers mingled with His prayers, I experienced a fantastic oneness with Him. This was an experience I enjoyed again and again each time the Spirit drew me into prayer. It is incredible when you think about it—prayer, in and of itself, is a spiritual and, therefore, a supernatural action. When we pray, we join Christ and enter into His prayers for us and others.

As I was drawn to my knees in prayer, the Spirit also drew me to Himself and filled my heart with the desire to lift worship to the Lord. With this action, by the Spirit, I recognized that worship has the power to motivate me to be thankful for the constant abiding of God through all seasons of my life. Regardless of the pain I feel in my body, regardless of my downcast emotional state, I can still choose to worship the Lord. And the act of worship itself can bring transformation to my thinking.

Today, I woke up with God breathing a scripture into my spirit and soul: "Goodness and mercy shall follow me all the days of my life, and I will dwell in the house of the Lord forever" (Psalm 23). I am grateful for that reminder in this season of struggle. It is a reminder that no pain, suffering, hopelessness, or frustration will remove me from God. His grace and love are a protective force that will keep me in His house forever. My meditation on that promise is so comforting. His goodness is so expansive.

My Prayer: I want to find complete joy and satisfaction in each moment, regardless of whether it is full, empty, happy, sad, giving, sterile, excellent, or boring. Would You, loving God, breathe life into those moments? Nothing needs to be void of Your presence and creative love. I worship You, Lord, and am so grateful that Your love is complete. It always brings good in every situation.

Will you pray: Lord, I worship You. Thank you for Your loving faithfulness. Thank you that Your plans for me are good, even when I can't see them.

Prayers of Worship

I enjoy spending part of my day outside, positioned on my favorite deck chair, as I view the display of natural beauty that inhabits my backyard. One week, I was forced to enjoy my garden in the early evening because it had been too hot to go outside during the day. I noticed something about the lily blossoms—they close in the evening! The Spirit reminded me that our hearts are like that flower.

When we look toward the Son, and He is shining down on us, the eyes of our hearts open, and we flourish. As we remove our heavenward glances, our hearts close. It is easy to turn away from Him when we are experiencing trials. The darkness may feel inviting because it is easier. But, if our hearts follow the darkness, they will soon shut... and the life we enjoy in the Spirit will wither.

Signs of life appear as we worship. Worship looks like the lily blossom in the sun—petals opened wide, drinking in the warmth and fully inviting it in. Having received the sun, it opens even further, and a dance between the Creator and His creation has begun—both enjoying the giving and receiving of life. Will you look to the Son today and let Him open the eyes of your heart? This is Jesus speaking:

"...true worshippers will worship the Father in spirit and truth; for the Father is seeking such to worship Him. God is Spirit, and those who worship Him must worship in spirit and truth" (John 4:23-24).

Worship is about who He is, not who I am. However, that truth is something we often have to remind ourselves of. As we experience the trials of life, we may not always *feel* like praising

God. I have discovered, however, that it is precisely the time we *need* to worship God. The love and compassion of God is a constant. He never changes, and what He has to give to us never changes. When we go through a trial, our negative thinking can pull us away from God. Nevertheless, if we choose to praise Him and rehearse His goodness, it can be the very thing we need to do to change our thinking. The constant love of God can be the grounding we need to pull us from negative thought patterns.

My prayer: Lord Jesus, I am so glad that You, Lord, are my constant God. Help me to remind myself that You are working Your good work in me even when I can't see it. Faith and trust in **who You are** become key to my ability to keep praying and believing. Thank You for Your Word, which paints a picture of Your faithfulness for me. Thank You for the many memories I possess of Your faithfulness extended towards me.

"...let us lay aside every weight, and the sin which so easily ensnares us, and let us run with endurance the race that is set before us, looking unto Jesus, the author and finisher of our faith..." (Hebrews 12:1-2).

Will you pray: Lord, help me to remember that Your timetable is so different from mine. I don't know what You have for me in the future, although I can be sure that Your plan for me is good. Living on this earth can narrow my vision, so I ask You to give me the eyes of the Spirit. I want Your will to be done in me and not my own. Work Your patience into my anxious heart and help me to run the race You have set before me.

Another prayer that aided in my ability to rest and wait on the Lord is meditation. I was introduced to this form of prayer through a church service that focused on what they called "soaking prayer." The body's posture was lying on the floor while your mind and heart were focused solely on being with the Lord and receiving what He had for you. Soaking was a good name for that prayer because the direction was to soak quietly in the Spirit of God. I initially began the practice because I wanted to dispel the anxiety that was building throughout this season of my life. I had been going through a dark time and was desperate to connect with God in a way that would lift my spiritual and emotional funk. I traveled to Canada, where I heard that revival was happening. And God did not disappoint.

The spiritual awakening I received at the church and my desperation for more of the same kept me engaged in the process when I traveled home. Morning and evening, I slid down to my favorite spot on the carpet to "soak" in God's Spirit. There were times when the presence of God was glorious and others when the only thing present was my anxious flesh yearning for the Spirit to fill me. I continued this practice for a year when I found that the peace, which was replacing my anxiety, alone was exhilarating. Still, I also found that my practice brought me greater intimacy and oneness with the Lord. I was amazed and delighted that that happened. The more I practiced my new form of prayer, the more I understood that God's love was faithful, regardless of whether I felt it.

Meditation teaches us to let go of our stress and the clutter in our minds and just sit with the Lord and take in His presence and love. Our minds and prayers can become caught up in either the future (what we desire to gain from God) or the past (what needs healing) when God wants to impart His love to us in the present moment. It is about "being" with God and not "doing." We don't need language when we are in our own state. Have you ever been with a friend or lover where you are both enjoying silence together? You can experience a special connection even without speaking a word. This is only a taste of what you can experience with the Lord as you explore the process of resting in the Spirit. The Word of God says, "Be still and know that I am God" (Psalm 46:10).

When you practice, find a place free of external noise. You can lie down or sit comfortably, play soft music, or sit in silence. If your mind starts chattering, gently shift it back to a peaceful place. I have also completed several oral guided meditations, which you can find on my podcast platform under "Unity with Christ."

God's directive to me in this season has been, "Slow down, pay attention to the now. Get your eyes focused on the small things you can accomplish each day. Don't long for the future or the past. Draw close to Me. Let My presence fill you."

As you begin your meditation practice, please be patient with yourself in this learning process. As long as I have practiced meditation, I am surprised by how much I still have to wrestle with my brain and bring it back from getting lost in the past or the future. Both of those places can be problematic when our focus remains stuck there. When focused on the past, we are usually giving place to pain and grief. Yes, it is important not to bury the past; however, if we lack the skill to adequately process the pain, the emotional pain can keep us from the peace and joy we can have in the present. The same struggle with our minds and emotions is true if we fix our attention on the future.

Fear and anxiety are usually the emotions that accompany that fixation. The only solution is learning to live in the now or in the present.

Jesus warns us, "Therefore, do not worry, saying, 'What shall we eat?' or 'What shall we drink?' or 'What shall we wear?' But seek first the kingdom of God and His righteousness, and all these things shall be added to you. Therefore, do not worry about tomorrow, for tomorrow will worry about its own things. Sufficient for the day is its own trouble" (Matthew 6:31,33-34 NKJ).

Jesus not only warns us about the stance we are to avoid, but He also instructs us concerning the stance we are to practice—and that is to be focused on the Lord. We can only obtain peace and joy by living in the present with our hearts and minds resting and trusting in Him. Only the Lord can heal the past wounds and manage our tomorrows. The Bible also reminds us that:

"The Lord's mercies...are new every morning" (Lamentations 3:22-23 NKJ). If what's ahead scares you and what's behind hurts you, then look above. God will not fail you.

Further instructions for meditative prayer are in my book Journey into Wholeness. My guided meditations are also on my podcast page, Unity with Christ.

Praying in the Holy Spirit

Do you know the Holy Spirit? He is the one who lives in you if you have given your life to Jesus. Nevertheless, have you met Him? Do you know that you can speak to Him? He is the One who empowers you to be like Christ. He is the same Spirit who empowered Christ. I have come to love the Holy Spirit. I have experienced His comfort, His strength, His peace. He is the One who leads and guides me. He is a very precious part of the Trinity. Will you reach out and get to know Him?

The Word of God tells us that it is through the Holy Spirit that we can know that we belong to God. "By this, we know that we abide in Him, and He in us, because He has given us of His Spirit" (I John 4:13 NKJ).

As believers in Christ, our journey is to be molded into His image daily. That is one of our main tasks here on earth. We are to be the picture of Christ to those who do not know Him. What an awesome but sometimes scary responsibility. It is only possible as we yield to the Holy Spirit. He, alone, can transform us and pour the love of God into these broken vessels so we can bring glory to God.

"For whom He foreknew, He also predestined to be conformed to the image of His Son...whom He called, these also He justified; and whom He justified, these He also glorified" (Romans 8:29-30 NKJ).

Regardless of whether we know Christ or not, we know that, on this earth, we will all experience trials. However, the exciting thing is that when we are in Christ, He promises to use everything for our good. That means our mistakes, sicknesses, persecutions, trauma—everything—can be turned around and used for God's glory and our good. That is an incredible promise: "And we know that all things work together for good to those who love God, to those who are the called according to His purpose" (Romans 8:28 NKJ).

One way we can act in agreement with the Holy Spirit is by yielding our plans for our future to God. His plan is the one that will be ultimately fulfilling. We can gain success in the world, but what God offers us far surpasses that worldly pursuit.

This is my prayer. Can you make it yours?

As I surrender my life to You, Spirit, reveal the more excellent plan You have for me. Help me to understand that You come to me not only for my benefit but to grant me the gifts I can use to work some of the same miracles that Jesus performed when He walked this earth: heal the sick, cast out demons, speak with other tongues, raise the dead and preach the gospel. Through the Spirit, we not only come to know the love of God for ourselves, but we are privileged to channel that love to others.

"As each one has received a gift, minister it to one another, as good stewards of the manifold grace of God" (I Peter 4:10 NKJ). Furthermore, as we practice that ministry and give the love of the Spirit to one another, that brings us full circle into the oneness God has for us and the whole body of Christ. This has been God's plan all along. As we come together, reflecting the goodness of God, God is then glorified through us. Jesus prays to the Father: "For the very glory you have given to me, I have given them so that they will be joined together as one and experience the same unity that we enjoy. You live fully in Me, and now I live fully in them" (John 17:22-23 PT).

Chapter Five
Our New Identity

How we see ourselves and how we see God:
Inside our journey to discover the heart of God and find our place in Him, there are growth steps that teach us "who God is" and how God views us. There can be distortions in our thinking that misinform us, and we need to be challenged to find oneness with God. There have been many, many times in my relationship with God that I have had to let go of my own views and beliefs and explore God's Word for the truth. The wonderful thing is that the Word of God never changes, and God never changes. When I would hit the rough patches in my recovery, remembering who God is and His faithful actions toward me gave me hope and the impetus to keep traveling.

I regard these two focal points, the way we view God and the way we view ourselves, as the foundation of our building intimacy with God. Suppose you are like me and found there were many years of living before coming to the Lord. In that case, you may have experienced many years of functioning from worldly pursuits, misbeliefs, and dysfunctional behaviors. All of the above can cloud our thinking and distance us from the knowledge of the true identities of God and self. The good news, however, is that the power of the Holy Spirit can correct all misperceptions if we ask Him. This healing is the heart of what is needed to align our views with Him.

You may be asking, "Where do I begin?" When we look back on our lives and seek to discover the wounds that have developed through the years, it can feel like a daunting task. The place to begin, however, is the present. When the wounds of the past have not been healed, the effects of those wounds bleed into the present. You may find that your relationships are not satisfying, you act out of anger and resentment instead of love, you may have developed addictions and poor habits that you can't seem to change, or you find that it is difficult to give yourself grace in your failures and forgive others for theirs. A good place to start is to pray this simple prayer.

Will you pray: Lord, I bring You the wounds of my past and the lies I believed about my own identity and Yours. Forgive me for the sinful ways I acted out of the misbeliefs. I need Your help with this season of change. I am aware that this transformation can't happen without You, and I am so very glad that You promised to perform this.

To attain oneness with God, we must come to Him with our true self, not our false self. What does that mean? Our true self is the identity founded and created by God. Take notice of the description of the true self vs. the false self:

True self

Emotions, Beliefs, Desires, Undeveloped abilities, Creativity, Unmet needs, Wounds, Need for God.
We can also label this self as our authentic self.

False Self

The Masks (Denial, Defense Mechanisms, Addictions, Withdrawal, Pride.)
We have created these masks to protect us
from the judgement by others.

Connecting with our true self can produce feelings of vulnerability, especially if the false self has been active for some time. This process, however, can be rewarding as you get in touch with the unburdened self. When we allow God to heal our wounds through the power of His Spirit, we will be able to present our authentic selves before the Lord. Our false self (unhealed) usually holds blockages to the Holy Spirit and in relationship to others.

If we choose to come into unity with Christ, we must allow ourselves to become vulnerable and drop the masks we have adopted to protect the fragile self. When we know that the Spirit of God covers us, there is no further need to self-protect. This can feel challenging, but if we remain connected to Him, He can bring us peace for our journey. Jesus finds unity when we are connected to our true selves.

From my experience with the Spirit, I can tell you that nothing is more fulfilling and exciting than giving the Spirit room to act. When Jesus is at the core of our being, influencing our minds, will, and emotions, we can stay true to who we are. Christ has created us. He formed us and gifted us with a specific plan meant for each one of us. He will guide us by His Spirit, and when we follow His directives, we align with who God intended us to be. We can speak and act from an authentic place—free from the need to create a new being out of the lusts of the flesh (worldly desires) or defenses, which mask the true self. To examine where you find yourself in your beliefs and actions surrounding your true and false self, ask yourself these questions:

- Perception of God: Can I see God as a good God? This is how I see God:

- Expectations: I know God will meet my needs. This is the need I am asking God for:

- True Self: These are the ways I am acting out of my true self:

- False Self (Misbeliefs/ Lie): These are the ways that I am hiding my true self:

- Truth: These are the ways I am believing and living in truth:

As I examine my authenticity in the now and what I want to bring to the Lord, this is what I discover:

- I want to love life—be content (thankful, joyful, peaceful) in all challenges and seasons.
- I want to walk through grief with grace—experience the sadness without getting stuck in self-pity.
- I want to accept the negative and positive parts of myself—embrace myself in the present before making future goals.
- I want to be honest about the things I can move forward with right now and the things I can't.
- I want to be able to face pain with no fear—only excitement to find a way through.
- I want to gain the ability to try a second time, a third

time, and a fourth.

You can see that my stance before God comes from an open and honest heart. This is a heart that God can answer.

My Prayer: Would You, loving God, breathe life into my desires (above)? My heart cannot fulfill those changes on its own. Help me to lean into Your amazing love and be transformed. I am so glad that You, Lord, are wedded to this process. That is why I choose to invite You right at the beginning of my challenge. I believe in the fulfillment of Your promise:

"Now may the God of peace who brought up our Lord Jesus from the dead...make you complete in every good work to do His will, working in you what is well pleasing in His sight, through Jesus Christ, to whom be glory forever and ever. Amen" (Hebrews 13: 20-21 NKJ).

Discovering our true selves and the wounds that have influenced the behaviors of our false selves can feel challenging, but I encourage you to take one step at a time.

Steps to becoming one with God:

1. Surrender your life to God's plan and direction: What area(s) of your life do you need to surrender to Him?

"Work out your own salvation with fear and trembling: for it is God who works in you both to will and to do for His good pleasure" (Philippians 2: 12-13 NKJ).

2. Know the character of God: What qualities of God's character do you want to embrace as your own?

"My flesh and my heart fail; but God is the strength of my heart and my portion forever" (Psalm 73: 26 NKJ).

3. Know how God sees me: What description from God do you want to apply to yourself?

"You are a chosen generation, a royal priesthood, His own special people...who once were not a people, but now the people of God..." (I Peter 2: 9-10 NKJ).

4. Learn who the Holy Spirit is: What names do you call Him?

This is Jesus speaking: "He who believes in Me, as the Scripture has said, 'out of his heart will flow rivers of living water,' but this He spoke concerning the Spirit, whom those believing in Him would receive" (John 7: 38-39 NKJ).

5. Join with God to share His love to others: What ways are you sharing?

Jesus spoke to His disciples, "Go therefore and make disciples of all the nations, baptizing them in the name of the Father and of the Son and of the Holy Spirit" (Matthew 28: 19 NKJ).

6. Join with the Spirit to fight the enemy: How do you fight the enemy?

"Oh, that My people would listen to Me, that Israel would walk in My ways! I would soon subdue their enemies and turn My hand against their adversaries" (Psalm 81: 13-14 NKJ).

7. Join with the Spirit to create a thankful heart: When circumstances are going well, it is easy to be thankful. The thing that the Lord was asking me to do, however, was to be thankful amid the struggle. What are you thankful for?

"Bless the Lord, O my soul, and forget not all His benefits: Who forgives all your iniquities, Who heals all your diseases" (Psalm 103: 2-3 NKJ).

It took me some time to shift my focus to the goodness of God and remind myself that He could bring the outcome to His liking. I could then be thankful for my illness, which taught me that I could be transformed and that dancing was not my whole identity. The pain taught me patience. The Holy Spirit empowered me to change in so many ways. I am grateful for my weakness, which propelled me to God. I am thankful to the Holy Spirit, who led me to school and chose me to bless others through my calling as a psychotherapist.

My prayer: Here is the prayer I prayed leading me into the heart of God and His plan for me. God used my weakness to move me into the blessing of God.

My Prayer
Bless me, Heavenly Father
Forgive my erring ways.
Grant me strength to serve Thee.
Put purpose in my days.
Give me understanding
Enough to make me kind.
So I may judge all people
With my heart and not my mind.
And teach me to be patient
In everything I do,
Content to trust Your wisdom
And follow after You.
And help me when I falter
And hear me when I pray.
Receive me in Thy kingdom
To dwell with Thee someday.
By Carol Romeo

Our soul comprises our mind, will, and emotions. Our emotions often become disrupted because we focus on the negative parts of our lives instead of the positive. When I can shift my focus to the goodness of God and become thankful for His work in my life, things begin to look a little rosier, and I find more peace in my soul.

"Think about things that are excellent and worthy of praise...and the God of peace will be with you" (Philippians 4: 8-9 NLT).

Chapter Six
Kingdom Living

Kingdom living is ushered in and maintained by the Holy Spirit. He is our teacher and the provider of the gifts that God is imparting to us. When Jesus calls us "His people," He calls us into His Kingdom. What does this look like? When God spoke to Moses, He declared, "'Now, therefore, if you will indeed obey My voice and keep My covenant, then you shall be a special treasure to Me, above all people; for all the earth is Mine. And you shall be to Me a kingdom of priests and a holy nation. These are the words which you shall speak to the children of Israel (Exodus 19:5-6 NKJ). '"

We are sent to reflect the Spirit to the world. We are not to receive the Spirit just for our own benefit but to also allow the Spirit to filter through us. Even though our surrender is personal (we are the ones who have to do the action), our actions are also universal. They can also benefit others. It is so amazing to me that when we choose to follow Him, He extends His Kingdom (which contains all healing, all righteousness, all holiness, all forgiveness, all glory) and delivers it to us. Heaven comes to earth when we are faithful to reach out to others and extend His

Kingdom to them. This is part of God's holy plan to spread His glory throughout the face of the earth. When we join with God's heart desires, we join with His Kingdom.

The phrase that the Lord has spoken to me lately is "higher and deeper, higher and deeper." Oh, how we love the high places! When we're sitting on the mountaintop with Jesus, we enjoy the shared intimacy with Him, with our Father and His precious Holy Spirit. We love to rehearse His truths, share the knowledge of the Kingdom, and exercise the authority given to us in that place. But what about the deep places? What transpires between God and us in those places?

Kingdom living is all about the highs and the lows. I think you will agree that we can't live on the mountaintop. We must go through the valleys so that we can grow. When our circumstances challenge us, we must press into the Lord to gain His strength and make the difficult choices ahead. Life is full of hills and valleys, but we can be sure that Jesus Christ is present at all times. Even the darkness cannot hide Him. This scripture was my life-line amid my deepest darkness:

"Even in the darkness, I cannot hide from You. To You, the night shines as day. Darkness and light are both alike to You" (Psalm 139: 12 NLT).

Here is the fruit produced in us as we embrace kingdom living: "...but we also glory in tribulations, knowing that tribulation produces perseverance; and perseverance, character, and character, hope. Now hope does not disappoint, because the love of God has been poured out in our hearts by the Holy Spirit who was given to us" (Romans 5: 3-5 NKJ).

My prayer: Lord Jesus, how I thank You for Your Sweet Spirit. I know I couldn't have stayed on this path with You without the love and strength of Your Spirit. From the first glorious infilling until today, You, Spirit, have been faithful. You strengthened me in my darkest days. How I love the many ways You have touched my body, soul, and spirit. You manifested the beauty and glory of Jesus Christ to me within our amazing companionship.

The key ingredient that kept me passionate and engaged in Kingdom living was (is) my spiritual hunger. You might ask, "What is it, Holy Spirit, that you have for me?" Our spiritual growth depends upon our hunger. How hungry are you? Jesus tells us that when we are hungry, we will be filled.

When we embrace the Kingdom, we are embracing the fullness of the Spirit. The Word of God instructs us, "But the manifestation of the Spirit is given to each one for the profit of all: for to one is given the word of wisdom through the Spirit, to another the word of knowledge through the same Spirit, to another faith by the same Spirit, to another gifts of healings by the same Spirit, to another the working of miracles, to another prophecy, to another discerning of spirits, to another different kinds of tongues, to another interpretation of tongues" (I Corinthians 12: 7-10 NKJ).

My experience with the gifts was plentiful. I jumped in with both feet. I was hungry for the more that God had for me. The Holy Spirit was, indeed, stirring my heart, and I was blessed to be in a church where the gifts of the Spirit were embraced. If you want my full story, read my book Expect the Miraculous. This season of my life was very exciting to me. My husband, Tony, and I were appointed elders in the church, so we prayed for parishioners at the end of each service.

Both Tony and I experienced many miraculous occurrences by the Holy Spirit. Personally, we both were delivered from alcohol addiction and smoking; I received an instantaneous back healing, and Tony heard the audible voice of God. As we prayed for others, we both had hearts and ears that were opened to the prayer coming from the Spirit. I also began going on excursions that I called "my mini ministry trips." I would start by praying for the Lord's direction. My travel log would remain open to wherever God would lead me. Here is one example:

I was planning a trip to drive from my home in La Crescenta to Palm Springs. When I started my drive, the Spirit told me that the Lord had a message for me; therefore, I listened more closely.

He instructed me to get off the freeway at the next rest stop, park, and wait for His next direction. I was already comfortable with this type of instruction, so I willingly followed His directive. As I sat in my car waiting for Him to explain His plan to me, the joy of the Lord flooded my heart. At that moment, I was fully aware that I would not want to be anywhere else. I was learning that traveling the pathway of God is more than exciting—it is jumping up and down exciting!! There is nothing else that can compare to it. The process of stepping into the heart of God and following the longings of God's heart is like stepping into the mysteries that dwell in the heart of the Kingdom. The mystery is brought into the light—be healed, have faith, be loved, be chosen, be righteous, be glorified, be filled (with the Spirit).

In the midst of my waiting, God spoke, "I want you to get out of the car and walk towards the wooded area. You will find the person I want you to speak to." I did as He directed and saw a young boy attempting to climb a tree. When I asked the Lord, "Is this who I am to speak to?" He, again, said, "wait." Just then, I saw a young adult woman running towards the boy, shouting his name. The Spirit signaled to me that this woman was the proposed individual I was waiting for.

I watched as this woman guided who I perceived to be her son over to the tables in the picnic area. I followed behind them, and when they were seated, I asked the woman if I could sit with them. She said, "Yes," and I sat beside her. Throughout the rest of our time together, I talked about life with Jesus. She already had some exposure to church but was excited to hear about the fullness of the Spirit that God had for her and her son. I had lunch (from a cooler in my car) that I shared with them, and I pointed them to some outside aids that could help them financially. I shared some cash with her to help with her immediate needs. I let her know how important she was to God and the detailed way that God had directed me to her.

It was obvious how blessed she was by my visit. I was blessed as well. It is always exciting to be used by God in that way. It is terrific/wonderful to not only view the supernatural movement of the Lord but also to be a part of it. This was just the beginning of my frequent mini-miracle trips. Present, in the gifts of the Spirit, is the authority we inherit from Jesus to perform the same miracles as He did when He walked the earth. The thing I needed to learn, however, is:

The gift is not the same as the giver of the gift.

Yes, being used by God is exciting. Participating in the health of others is exciting. Nevertheless, the focus of our worship needs to be Jesus (the giver of the gift) and not the gift. Jesus is the only One worthy of our praise. The gifts come to us through the authority of Jesus Christ when He purchased our freedom at the cross. It is by His grace that He passes to us His authority to minister in His name. It is by the name of Jesus that we can:

Heal the sick, deliver the oppressed, raise the dead, preach righteousness (Matthew 10: 8).

My concern for you is: As you minister under the power of the Spirit, remember that the gifts come through the Creator of the gifts. I realize, through experience, how easy it can be to get caught up in the excitement of the gift and forget to thank the Giver of the gift. Our focus on the gifts can lead us to misguided attention to the gifts and even a form of worship towards them. What is the intention of your heart as you practice your gift? Ask yourself if you are ministering from the flesh, thereby producing pride. Ask yourself if you are glorifying God through your gift. Glorifying God needs to be the primary intention of our hearts. Here is a poem that can help you to focus on worship:

Worship the Three in One
Lord, I come before Thee
To Worship at Thy tent
How I thank Thee, Father,
For riches to me sent.
No one but Thine alone
Is worthy of my praise.
Lifting my heart to Thee,
To Thee my voice I raise.
Christ the Lord is coming
As King for all to see.
Worshipping forever
The Son who died for me.
Glory to the Spirit;
I'm filled with His great love.
Flood me with Your presence,
Visit me from above.
How I bless Thee, Spirit,
The Father and the Son.
Bowing my heart to Thee,
I praise Thee, Three in One.
By Carol Romeo

If you like this poem, I have more poems in my book
Meditations from the River. I also have oral guided meditations
on my podcast page under Unity with Christ.

73

Epilogue

As I close this book, I am excited to share the truths that the Holy Spirit has brought His light into with each of you. I encourage you to explore my challenges to you and use the Holy Spirit to unfold to you, personally, what He has for you in this season. Coming into oneness with Jesus is a hefty goal, but one that I know the Spirit will help you with. I pray that as you work through some of my suggestions, you will find the unity with Jesus you have longed for. "I am in you, Jesus, and you are in me" is my heart's prayer for you and me. It is also Christ's prayer for each of you. We are Christ's creation, and His promises will never fail us. They are all Amen. And So Be It.

"...and He died for all, that those who live should live no longer for themselves, but for Him who died for them and rose again...Therefore, if anyone is in Christ, he is a new creation; old things have passed away; behold, all things have become **new**" (2 Corinthians 5: 15 &17 NKJ).

For all things Carol visit:
AuthorCarolRomeo.com

Special thanks to

Bob Anderson & Ernest Joy
For editing and publishing support.

www.ingramcontent.com/pod-product-compliance
Lightning Source LLC
Chambersburg PA
CBHW072034150726
47999CB00002B/908